YOU ARE HIS

CLAIMING WHO YOU ARE
BECAUSE OF WHOSE YOU ARE

CAROL BEVIL

WESTBOW
PRESS®
A DIVISION OF THOMAS NELSON
& ZONDERVAN

WestBow Press books may be ordered through booksellers or by contacting:

WestBow Press
A Division of Thomas Nelson & Zondervan
1663 Liberty Drive
Bloomington, IN 47403
www.westbowpress.com
844-714-3454

Scripture quotations taken from The Holy Bible, New International Version® NIV® Copyright © 1973 1978 1984 2011 by Biblica, Inc. TM. Used by permission. All rights reserved worldwide.

Scripture quotations marked (NLT) are taken from the Holy Bible, New Living Translation, copyright © 1996, 2004, 2007 by Tyndale House Foundation. Used by permission of Tyndale House Publishers, Inc., Carol Stream, Illinois 60188. All rights reserved.

Photography: Mo Davis Photography, @modavisphotography
https://modavisphotography.com/.

@fuelbodyfeedsoul fuelbodyfeedsoul.com.

ISBN: 978-1-6642-1030-1 (sc)
ISBN: 978-1-6642-1029-5 (hc)
ISBN: 978-1-6642-1068-4 (e)

Library of Congress Control Number: 2020921360

Print information available on the last page.

WestBow Press rev. date: 11/09/2020

To:

From:

Date:

For God: Thank You for pursuing me relentlessly. I pray everything in my life points to you.

For my three daughters: I pray they always look to Jesus for their true reflections and grow to be the P31 women God made them to be.

For all the women I am blessed to coach and know: I pray we stand in God's truth about who we are, how we were made, and what we are uniquely gifted to do for the kingdom.

CONTENTS

INTRODUCTION

I came to faith as a Martha ...

After I surrendered my life to Jesus, I still wrestled with the sense that I just wasn't doing this life thing right. At church and in small groups or Bible studies, my "newness" just solidified my sense of inadequacy. Why didn't God make me patient, soft-spoken, and ... well, "soft" is the only word that comes to mind. For years, this feeling of inadequacy built walls in my faith life: "Prayer isn't my gift"; "Sharing my faith with others isn't my gift"; and 100 percent, "Patience is *not* my gift." So I dug into my inner Martha. I was determined to work hard and be the best mom, best wife, best friend, and well, the best Christian. Unfortunately, the more I toiled, the less peace I felt. See, I couldn't understand where Martha went wrong. She was hospitable and made sure Jesus's needs were met. So I was always confused as to why "sitting still" Mary was the "good" sister? Is there a preferred kind of service—feet washing, not dishwashing? I felt Martha's resentment in my bones; church made me feel surrounded by Marys. I felt the torn veil closing and growing thicker. My faith felt fragile and dim. I was deep in the briar patch. I asked a friend to pray for my faith. (Yep, remember prayer wasn't my gift; ugh, it hurts to write that). My friend then asked me a tough, humbling question: When you read about Martha and Mary, do you listen to Jesus or yourself?

Martha wasn't doing anything wrong. Her hospitality was authentic. She was eager to invite Jesus into her home and feed Him. However, my understanding of this story was focused on the wrong end of things! I wasn't focused on Jesus. I was comparing myself to Mary. Just. Like. Martha. Even though I believed and decided to follow Jesus, my behavior hadn't changed. I still relied on my own efforts and sought the world's opinion of those efforts to define me. No wonder I felt inadequate, resentful, and exhausted. See, what I missed in the story was Jesus's response to the frustrated Martha. He doesn't respond to Martha with anger. No. He *knows* exactly who she is and meets her there. He knows she welcomed Him, sought His wisdom in the face of her resentment and frustration (gotta love her chutzpah), and trusted His love. Jesus acknowledges her troubles. Then He gently and lovingly tells her she is focused on the wrong things. Jesus is the one thing. When you focus on Jesus first, seek to know God's truth, the more you experience the sufficiency of God's grace. The beautiful mystery of an intimate relationship with God is knowing that even in your weakness, He is made strong. When you believe God is who He says He is, trust Him with your identity. Then you can be the light He made you to be!

I love that the next time Martha encounters Jesus, she is still the Marthaest of all Marthas. She marches out to Jesus in full chutzpah: "If you had been here, my brother would not have died." He gently reminds her of who He is. Then she argues about rolling away the stone because Lazarus is going to smell. He reminds her again of her belief. Jesus needs Martha to be Martha! Through Martha I learned that Jesus will always remind me to get out of my own way and trust that He is the one thing.

Through Martha I learned that Jesus knows exactly who I am but still loves me.

Digging into God's Word to learn His truth about Martha led me to find as many verses as I could where God reminds me who I am to Him. As a personal trainer and nutrition and cycling coach, I spend a lot of time with women who have allowed the mirror, the scale, social media, their own efforts, and other people's opinions to diminish who they are. The enemy uses culture and the world to steal and destroy our God-given light. I've learned that no matter the approval, and even if you reach whatever worldly goal you chase if you don't seek God first you will always feel less than. Worse, your true identity is at risk. When you trust who He is and whose you are, you experience the abundant, peace-filled joy God desires for you no matter your circumstance.

This twenty-one-day book comes from those verses I've prayed to anchor my identity—and now my daughters—firmly in God. Over the years I return to these verses when I feel the enemy using my doubts, shortcomings, and anxiety to tear down my God-given worth. I look to Him to find myself. I am grateful that I can sit at His feet and hear His truth over and over. I pray these verses over my children and my husband. I pray these verses over my friends and clients. I pray these verses anchor you when you doubt, feel inadequate, or are filled with anxiety. I pray these verses lead you to see God first in every area of your life.

God created you in His image. You are fully known to Him. You are His treasured possession exactly the way you are. You are His.

CHOSEN

They will wage war against the Lamb, but the
Lamb will triumph over them because he is
Lord of lords and King of kings—and with him
will be his called, chosen and faithful followers.

—Revelation 17:14

I love this verse, in particular, "and with him will be his called, chosen and faithful followers." God does not need me, but He chose me. He chose *you*. Isn't our desire to be chosen at the heart of almost everything we want? We are hardwired to feel wanted and necessary. In fact, God designed you as an empty vessel with an extraordinary need: the need to desire Him. As kids, we desperately want to be picked. As adults, we want to be chosen by the college, the sorority, the employer, and the man or woman. We tie so much of our self-worth to being chosen. But here is your forever good news—truly the best news—you, my friend, are chosen. You have been picked by God to be on the ultimate team: Jesus's. He called you, and you answered yes! Your role is to faithfully follow by living out your calling through ignited faith, bringing Him glory so that others will choose to join His team.

No one knows your heart's desire better than God. He understands that humans crave feeling wanted and needed. Knowing this, perhaps one of the Bible's most beautiful binding threads, which runs from Genesis to Revelation, is its love story: the love God has for His creation, the love He has for His people, and the love He wants you to show others. God isn't shy about His love for you. He affirms your importance to Him over and over. He chose you before you were born (Jeremiah 1:5). He gave His Son (John 17:6) to cover you in His righteousness despite your brokenness and rebellion so He could be with you. As well, your heavenly Father wants you to rest securely in the knowledge that you are wanted and needed by Him (Genesis 28:15; Psalm 94:14; Romans 8:38–39). You can trust that once you have been chosen, God will never forsake you.

The beauty of being chosen by God is not only that His love for you is perfect and trustworthy, but also the more you surrender to this unfathomable love, the more you feel wanted and needed. It is important to note that God's love does not set you above anyone else. Rather, being chosen is a call to humble obedience; it is a call to love others as you are loved. It is a call to boast of God, not of self; it is a call to give your best to the team so that your life brings God glory. And there is no need to fret that you aren't doing enough or worry that God will send you packing when you mess up; remember His promise to never forsake you. You can find peace in the fact that being chosen does not come from you but is because of Him. No matter how far you wander, once you are chosen, like a good shepherd, God will relentlessly pursue you.

So when the enemy, the world, and your flesh are set against you, remember *you are chosen*. God pointed His finger at you and called your name. The moment you surrendered to His call and gave your life to Jesus, the Holy Spirit took up residence. You now wear the jersey of His truth and His victory. You do not enter the battlefield alone because within you is the Spirit of power, peace, and self-control. You are now a living testimony for God's saving grace, infinite mercy, and unfathomable love.

Remember:
There is "no power of hell nor scheme of man" that can ever pull you from the steadfast love of God.

You, my friend, are chosen.

Reflection They will wage war against the Lamb, but the Lamb will triumph over them because he is Lord of lords and King of kings—and with him will be his called, chosen and faithful followers. (Revelation 17:14)

_____

_____

_____

_____

_____

_____

_____

_____

_____

_____

_____

_____

_____

_____

DAY 2

WORTHY

The Lord your God is with you, the Mighty
Warrior who saves. He will take great delight
in you; in his love he will no longer rebuke
you, but will rejoice over you with singing.
—Zephaniah 3:17

In the months after my baptism at the age of forty, I found
comfort in the Old Testament. Suddenly, with fresh eyes and
a softened heart, I found Jesus on every page. And for the first
time as well, my heart knew God's Word breathed; it was a
living how-to manual for my life. Several years later, knowing
my newfound unquenchable thirst for God's Word but also
my insecurity with how to approach it, a dear friend (isn't it
fabulous how God places exactly who we need in our lives
when we need them?) gave me a set of verse cards. The verse
cards were personalized. For example, Zephaniah 3:17 read,

> The Lord your God is with you, (insert your name),
> the Mighty Warrior who saves. He will take great
> delight in you, (insert name); in His love He will no

longer rebuke you, (insert name), but will rejoice
over you, (insert name) with singing.

These personalized verse cards taught me that the Bible is not
only a how-to manual but also a love letter from my heavenly
Father. A love letter from your Father to *you*. Through His
Word, God's constant desire is for each of us to see ourselves
through His eyes so that we are armed against the world and the
enemy who seek to destroy our worth. What better and simpler
reminder of our worth than in Zephaniah 3:17?

Now I understand that in Zephaniah, God is delighting in Israel,
but I am Israel. *You* are Israel. God delights in you. His love is
so complete that His joy bubbles up and overflows; it simply
cannot be contained. He rejoices over you with singing! All
that is to say to hold Zephaniah 3:17 close. Memorize it. Pray it.
Make it your screen saver. The world and the enemy relentlessly
work to destroy and steal your joy by undermining your worth
(spend a few minutes scrolling). The book of Zephaniah, like all
of God's Word, is armor. It reminds you that with God, you are
never alone. He is your "mighty warrior." In Zephaniah, you
know the truth of your worth; the Creator of heaven and earth
steadfastly loves you. He takes such delight in who He created
you to be that He rejoices and sings over you!

So the next time the world and the enemy try to knock you
down, remember your worth to the God who knows every
hair on your head and placed it there. Allow Zephaniah 3:17 to
be His constant lullaby in your ear, soothing you during any
struggle.

Let Him whisper the truth in your ear:
**"You are of such worth that
you are My delight."**

Reflection The Lord your God is with you, the Mighty Warrior who saves. He will take great delight in you; in his love he will no longer rebuke you, but will rejoice over you with singing. (Zephaniah 3:17)

_____

_____

_____

_____

_____

_____

_____

_____

_____

_____

_____

_____

_____

DAY 3

WONDERFULLY MADE

For you created my inmost being; you
knit me together in my mother's womb.
I praise you because I am fearfully and
wonderfully made; your works are
wonderful, I know that full well.

—Psalm 139:13–14

This verse is a vital daily part of my professional life as I coach women. Well at least the professional life I finally embraced—speaking God's truth into the arena of the fitness and wellness industry. I am a certified personal trainer and nutrition coach. For decades, I am ashamed to admit, I was part of my industry's problematic message that beauty is tied to fitness and weight. I am not suggesting that I was a drill sergeant–type of coach. My personality is to motivate, encourage, and inspire people to achieve more than they thought possible. Nevertheless, I peddled the lies of my industry because I did not see my or my clients' beauty and worth through God's eyes. I believed in the mirror, the scale, and the world as the arbiters of beauty and happiness. I coached worldly transformation achieved solely through willpower, restriction, and no pain, no gain exercise. I coached my clients to be self-reliant and to invest their time and money chasing superficial, often joy-robbing, change.

I had no idea how much my worldly view must have been breaking God's heart. Even unaware, the truth is I was a part of the enemy's schemes to claim people's identities through their weight and the false idol of the diet and wellness culture. But God, God broke in and revealed the truth to me. His call for us to be good stewards of His creation—our bodies included—is not a call to put His creation above our relationship with Jesus. Rather, its wonder is to direct our reverence toward God. My relationship with Jesus opened my eyes. I am no longer a part of the diet culture mindset but coach the development of a kingdom mindset. I am called to help my clients pursue a Romans 12:2 transformation by seeking God first in all things. It is only through the renewal of our minds and the transformed desires of our hearts that we each come to know the truth and begin to honor our bodies as God intended. We are wonderfully and fearfully made.

So let me repeat this for those in the back:
You are wonderfully made!

Do you speak this truth over yourself? Or do you put yourself down and find every perceived physical fault? Do you allow the enemy to destroy your peace through which you build up the false idol of diet culture, fitness, and self-care at the expense of your relationship with Jesus? Do you know that the diet culture is an anchor pulling you downward and inward through fear and false worship? Bound by guilt and shame? Do you know that God calls you only to fear and worship Him? Do you know that Jesus bore your guilt and took your shame? The enemy uses the worldly focus on superficial beauty standards, which change to the whims of trend, not only to destroy your peace, but to steal you from God's greater purpose for your life.

God knew how we would struggle with our body images and self-worth, so He constantly reminds us that we are "beautiful," a royal priesthood," and "His treasured possession." Unfortunately, through culture the enemy twists God's truth, causing us to focus too much of our energy on physical appearance. We turn honoring our bodies, being their stewards, self-discipline, and moderation into vanity, self-loathing, shame, willfulness, guilt, and idolatry. We empower the enemy to twist God's wonderful into ashes. The fruit of the lies of diet culture is apparent; it is not well with our souls or our physical and emotional health. The more we turn from God's truth to the world's lies in this arena, the less we are able to be used for His glory. Outsideour own false worship of fitness and wellness, just think how our focus on physical appearance causes us to judge others.

You are not only wonderfully made (yes, physically because God doesn't make mistakes), you are enough; you are fearfully made! God not only uniquely designed you exactly as He desired so that you can fulfill His purpose and bring Him glory but to know from birth to grave that you belong to Him. You are the pinnacle of His creation and His image bearer on earth. The wonder of your body and its capabilities should be awe-inspiring; it should lead to reverence for the One who created it. It should lead us to deeply desire God and praise Him. The wonder of your body should not draw you inward and drag you downward but point you outward and upward to God.

Romans 12:2 tells us transformation is a mind and a heart that sets God above everything and through which we receive "all the things" (my favorite expression that my friend Kerri says). All the things from God—just to name a few—are peace, joy, blessings, assurance, forgiveness, redemption, strength, a grateful heart, righteousness, self-control, and freedom. Freedom to know full well that you are wonderfully made so you can get busy fulfilling God's will for your life!

Reflection For you created my inmost being; you knit me together in my mother's womb. I praise you because I am fearfully and wonderfully made; your works are wonderful, I know that full well. (Psalm 139:13–14)

HIS MASTERPIECE

For we are God's handiwork, created in
Christ Jesus to do good works, which
God prepared in advance for us to do.
—Ephesians 2:10

You are God's handiwork. His workmanship. His artwork. Think about that for a minute. Actually, think about that biblical truth for a good long while. God, the greatest artist of all time, chose to create you! Exactly as you are. No detail mistaken. Every part of you was created gifted and imbued with a God-given purpose. Every facet of what and who you are is designed to be a specific part of God's perfect plan. Only you, in all your broken imperfections, can fulfill what God specifically calls you to do. In other words, you are necessary, needed, and desired by God. So the next time you speak harsh words to and about yourself, remember you are criticizing God's perfect masterpiece. Truly every hair on your head that isn't curly or straight or blonde or brown enough for you is exactly as God desired and needed it to be. Of course the beautiful, deeper mystery of this verse, as Paul teaches the Ephesians about salvation through grace and faith, is its bold assertion that you were predestined to be a part of God's plan.

Predestination is such a difficult concept for me. Before I was saved, God knew? Before I was even a thought God knew I would fall on my knees at forty and beg Jesus to be the Lord of my life? Look, I will always grapple with this idea, but what I've come to understand is that my salvation cannot and was not earned by me—or my actions—being perfect. Rather, by becoming new in Christ through a salvation that I do not deserve (hello, grace), the Holy Spirit continuously works to transform my inward desires so that I work for the good of God. God knows my every imperfection and will equip me to do His will. In other words, God doesn't call me to change myself but to trust that He covered my brokenness and will transform me to use me for His glory.

My somewhat aha moment with Ephesians 2:10 came in an ordinary bedtime conversation with one of my kids. She was in the "leave the light on" stage. We talked about how her nightlight destroys the scary darkness and reveals that what we fear may be of our own imagination and come from within us. As we sat there, enjoying the protective warmth of a little bit of light in her room, I thought about how light and dark coexist but cannot be part of each other. How the light causes the darkness to recede. God is light! When you give your life to Christ, the light switch in your heart is switched on. The more you seek His light, the more the darkness within you gives way. The more you desire to do good. The more you begin to recognize that you are indeed His masterpiece. The best part is that when you're lost, uncertain, scared, or filled with self-recrimination, Ephesian 2:10 reminds you of whose you are and that He is working for and through you now and even before you were formed.

Ephesians 2:10 transforms the Christian from religion to relationship. Living Ephesians 2:10 is to embrace the radical, rich, deep blessings that God wants to lavish upon you. It is the light switch that reveals, "the peace that surpasses all understanding." It is the light switch that allows our eyes to see the depth of God's love for us, a love that pursues us, a love that knows us (yep, the warts too). It is the light switch that bathes us in His unfathomable grace and forgiveness. It is the light switch that not only chases worry, shame, and guilt out of the room but ignites your inner fire to pursue God's purpose for your life. Ephesians 2:10 is the light switch that reveals the truth: You are God's masterpiece.

Reflection For we are God's handiwork, created in Christ Jesus to do good works, which God prepared in advance for us to do. (Ephesians 2:10)

_____

_____

_____

_____

_____

_____

_____

_____

_____

_____

_____

_____

HIS TEMPLE

Do you not know that your bodies are
temples of the Holy Spirit, who is in you,
whom you have received from God? You are
not your own; you were bought at a price.
Therefore honor God with your bodies.
—1 Corinthians 6:19–20

Raised Jewish, my biblical perspective is often through the lens of the Old Testament. Not just because it was the Bible I knew as a kid, but part of my testimony was a challenge to find Jesus on every page in the Old Testament. And once I decided to look for Him, there He was! Despite my heritage, every time I read the Bible, I just dread Leviticus: Ugh. I pray, "God help me focus. Keep me from skipping and skimming. Help me know that *all* of Your Word is profitable for teaching." However, this past year was different. Not the dread of having to read Leviticus or my prayer. Leviticus is Leviticus. This year, however, when I started to skim, the Spirit whispered, "Details, Carol. Details." So I stopped, closed my eyes, and said, "Okay God, I will embrace the details." Here are some of my notes.

In the desert, despite their constant whining and disobedience, God's Spirit stayed with the Jews. His Spirit was among them. Separate but present. His Spirit rested in the Holy of Holies, within the inner sanctum of the tabernacle and central to the tribes of Israel. God's plan was not just to free the Jews from slavery but to renew their minds and transform their hearts to seek Him first, to trust Him, and to be His people.

In the midst of God's transformation of the Jews from slave to His, God gives an account of every minute detail of the tabernacle's construction— down to the color of the thread to be used— as well as its symbolic contents and the laws regarding entering and worshipping. But why? Why account every boring (I said what I said) detail of the tabernacle's construction and then repeat it a lot? God is intentional. He is purposeful in His decision to account for every detail and the repetition of each facet. My dad always taught me when someone repeats something, listen because it's important. Okay God, Why? Why would You include the tabernacle's construction in such repetitious detail? What am I missing?

So I prayed. And I read it again (hear the most exasperated tone you can imagine).

Within the laborious details of Leviticus, I believe God reveals our worth within the scope of His creation. It reveals His unfathomable love for His people and the faithfulness of His covenant. It reveals His desire to be with us and His constant mercy. It reveals His character. He is a God who stays. His Spirit, despite their willful disobedience, never abandons His chosen people. He is a God who completely loves. He protects, provides, guides, corrects, and instructs. He is a merciful God. He is righteous and must judge their sins, but His heart is ever inclined to mercy and forgiveness. Leviticus's focus on the tabernacle looks forward to the coming of Christ as well; it is a glimpse into God's ultimate plan for grace. In the desert, God is *among* His people. His Spirit is centrally present but separate; it is behind the veil, cloaked in mystery, and protected behind ritual and law. Jesus will once and for all tear this veil. Through Christ, God is no longer among us but *within* us. We are no longer held separate, distanced by ritual and law. Rather, we can directly honor God through an intimate relationship with Him. God's grace and Christ's obedience transformed the tabernacle into you. Now *you* are His temple.

Leviticus is in part a book about God's loving attention for you. Every detail of you was knit together and fashioned by God. Important. Special. Purposed. There is not a hair on your head that He does not know. He knows the sound and cadence of your voice, the hue of your skin, the set of your jaw, the desires of your heart, and the thoughts in your head. He knows your strengths and your weaknesses. He built you strong and beautiful, and He filled you with His empowering Spirit. You are anointed and chosen, His special treasure. You must wander the desert of this fallen world, but know that God has set you apart. You are not alone. His Spirit is within you to be an ever-present protector, provider, guide, helper, and teacher. As God's temple, you are called to honor Him through what you allow to enter. Guard your temple. The enemy seeks to corrupt God's temple. So guard what enters through your eyes, your ears, and your mouth (my dad would say what comes out too). Protect the intimate relationship you have been gifted through Christ. Be God's temple, a living testament to His glory.

God's grace and Christ's obedience transformed the temple into you.

Reflection Do you not know that your bodies are temples of the Holy Spirit, who is in you, whom you have received from God? You are not your own; you were bought at a price. Therefore honor God with your bodies. (1 Corinthians 6:19–20)

_____

_____

_____

_____

_____

_____

_____

_____

_____

_____

_____

_____

_____

_____

DAY 6

HIS CHILD

So you are no longer a slave, but God's
child; and since you are his child,
God has made you also an heir.

—Galatians 4:7

As a mom, this verse makes my heart swell. Though I never thought I wanted to get married or have kids (my dog was awesome), the love a parent has for a child is, well, indescribable. Seriously, no matter how much they make you crazy (yeah, that aspect of parenting is indescribable too), the love remains acute and steadfast. You want to bear their every hurt, physical and emotional. When they succeed, it makes you happier than when you have your own success. It's an overwhelming, breathtaking love that burrows deep into the marrow of your bones. It's a love that resolutely stands firm in the midst of heartbreaking, infuriating disobedience. It's a love that steadfastly hopes.

God did not rescue His people from Egypt or you from the grave because He wanted to prove His power and His omnipotence. He rescued you from your physical, emotional, and spiritual enslavement because you are His child. I cannot imagine the depth of God's love for His children, but oh how grateful I am for it. I cannot imagine the love Jesus had for His Father and for His Father's children. But I know I want to live a life that reflects that love. I want to live a life that daily proclaims my identity as God's child and heir.

Of all the identities you can ascribe to yourself (lawyer, mother, sister, wife), the identity I hope you claim and proclaim most fervently is "I am a Child of God." Who you are must be rooted in the unchanging, eternal love of God. He created you in His image. He knit you together and knew you before you were a thought. He set you apart from the rest of His creation. He chose to love you so deeply—despite your sin nature—that He sacrificed His only Son to restore you to your true identity: His child and heir. His love for you is overwhelming, a steadfast love that is filled with the hope of you. In God, through Jesus, you have a Father who rescues you (even from yourself), carries not only your every hurt but bore the full weight of your sin and celebrates your every success. As God's child, know you have a loving Father who wants good for you and who eagerly anticipates your return home to Him.

In the last days of my dad's life, he told me I was the apple of his eye. Oh, the love that washed over me and ran through me in that moment. In that simple, old-fashioned phrase, I knew my dad's love was not only constant but complete. You are the apple of God's eye. He fully knows you yet still fully loves you. You are His beloved child. Let your heart swell in that simple truth.

Of all the identities you claim, I hope you claim and proclaim most fervently, "I am a child of God."

Reflection So you are no longer a slave, but God's child; and since you are his child, God has made you also an heir. (Galatians 4:7)

_____

_____

_____

_____

_____

_____

_____

_____

_____

_____

_____

_____

_____

_____

DAY 7

HIS DELIGHT

You will be a crown of splendor in the Lord's
hand, a royal diadem in the hand of your
God. No longer will they call you Deserted,
or name your land Desolate. But you will
be called Hephzibah, and your land Beulah,
for the Lord will take delight in you.

—Isaiah 62:3–5

I often think as a coach about Genesis 1:27: "So God created
man in His own image; in the image of God He created him."
The more time I spend in God's Word, the more I come to
understand that each word is divinely inspired and perfect. It
is not a whim or poetic flourish when God tells us that we are
"made in His image." We are a reflection of all that He is. As
a mom, I think about how God must feel toward His beloved
creation. So often when my kids are struggling, I have said,
"If only you could see yourself through my eyes." When I am
struggling, I know God pleads the same truth to me as His
child. Isaiah 62 holds a special place in my heart as a parent and
as one of God's children. It is the constant, present reminder by

my loving Father: "if only you could see all that you are to me. If only you could see all that I made you to be.

Do you know that God speaks the same truth to you? Do you know that you are beloved? Do you know He sees you through the eyes of a loving father? Sure, He is all-knowing and sees the truth of you. He knows your sin and your weaknesses. He knows every hair on your head and every thought within it. He knows all that you believe to be worse about yourself. But He loves you completely. He loves you perfectly. His heart breaks every time you trade who you were made to be for the ashes of this world. So like any good father, when you struggle or falter, He lovingly reminds you of who you are:

You are a crown of splendor.
A royal diadem.

And your Father delights in you.

As a crown and a royal diadem, you are significant and beautiful. In the world, these objects are used to set apart those who are divinely chosen by God. You, my beautiful friend, are as precious and beautiful to your Father as crown jewels. He sets you apart as chosen. And if there is any doubt how He delights in you, *all* of you, then look to the word "hephzibah." Hephzibah is a name of endearment and means "my delight is in her." He calls you the source of His delight. When the enemy whispers lies in your ear, hear God's truth: "Child, if only you could see all that I see in you. You are a priceless treasure that I hold in my hand. Know that your current state or circumstance is vapor. Know that you are a source of delight, set apart, chosen, favored, and blessed."

Isaiah 62 celebrates your worth to God. Do not trade your God-given beauty for the world's ashes. Do not allow circumstances to diminish your God-given light. Shine like the precious creation you were made to be. Shine like ones who know God delights in them. Shine so brightly that you magnify Christ. Shine in a way that no one who encounters you can deny that God is glorious. You are God's crown and diadem. When you see yourself through His love, your life will proclaim His greatness and the immeasurable worth of His grace through Jesus Christ.

Reflection You will be a crown of splendor in the Lord's hand, a royal diadem in the hand of your God. No longer will they call you Deserted, or name your land Desolate. But you will be called Hephzibah, and your land Beulah, for the Lord will take delight in you. (Isaiah 62:3–5)

_____

_____

_____

_____

_____

_____

_____

_____

_____

_____

_____

_____

BEAUTIFUL

You are altogether beautiful, my
darling, beautiful in every way.
—Song of Songs 4:7

How often do you look in a mirror and see yourself through God's eyes? How often do you remember and give thanks that your outer reflection was made in the image of God? He crafted every detail exactly the way He desired. Not only is there no flaw about you, but you are "altogether beautiful." Look, I get that Song of Songs celebrates the gift of covenant love between a man and a woman, but I want you to know that this Word also celebrates the wondrous beauty of God's creation: You.

You are beautiful, lovingly created by a God who makes no mistakes. I know, I know what you are thinking, *Sure Carol, I get that my beauty comes from within … but I am judged—goodness, if truth be told, I judge myself—based on the scale, the size of my jeans, what I see in the mirror, and by culture's standards.* As a mom to three daughters, I understand the futility of telling someone she is beautiful to God. Despite arming my girls with verses that truthfully define beauty, they often dissolve in tears and reply, "Mom, I *know* God thinks I'm beautiful. And you *have* to say I'm beautiful. But the world doesn't agree. I'm too tall. My stomach is too fat. My skin is too broken out." In other words, my girls—and no doubt many of you reading this—don't want to hear about "true" beauty. They want the superficial, subjective, worldly beauty that inundates their social media and is marketed. They want what most of us want: beauty that can be measured, reflected in the mirror, and is admired by others.

I know the cost of this desire. Decades in the fitness and wellness industry have taught me the moment my girls—or any women— enter the enemy's battlefield and fight by his rules, they have already lost the war. He will give them wins along the way just to keep them enslaved to the desire to measure up to whatever the world defines as beautiful. He will diminish their God- given beauty so slowly that they never become fully aware of the collateral damage and its costs: peace with themselves; their self-esteem; their physical, emotional, and mental health; money; marriage; friendships; fellowship; their joy and precious time with their heavenly Father. The enemy is successfully distracting us by twisting the definition of what we call beautiful from God's truth to the world's trends. The ultimate cost, and what the enemy is after, is our identities as daughters of the King.

So we, Christian sisters, right here and right now need to stand firm. We must rebuke the enemy: "My outward appearance is beautiful in every way. Not in part but altogether. The whole!" The definition of outward (yep, the superficial, look in the mirror beauty) can never be found in the world's mirror even if you reach whatever ideal it is you seek. Beauty is found through God's eyes and is revealed in His Word. There are two things, my beautiful sister, that you must cling to. First, you are in this world but not of it. Second, when you struggle to wrestle free from the enemy's lies about your beauty, run to the cross, and surrender your worry to God because He will open your eyes to the truth.

You are beautiful.

PS. And can we just accept here today that your outward beauty is not fleeting? You are beautiful today. You grow more beautiful as you age. You grow more beautiful the more brightly you shine in the knowledge of God.

Reflection   You are altogether beautiful, my darling, beautiful
in every way. (Song of Songs 4:7)

_____

_____

_____

_____

_____

_____

_____

_____

_____

_____

_____

_____

KNOWN

You know when I sit and when I rise; you
perceive my thoughts from afar. You discern
my going out and my lying down; you are
familiar with all my ways. Before a word is on
my tongue you, Lord, know it completely.

—Psalm 139:2–4

We live in a world where we can easily manipulate our images and who we want people to think we are: happily married, financially set, amazing parents, well-traveled, fit, charitable. There are even photo filters that allow us to enhance or change our appearances. We live in a world where one's image is everything. We've become a culture of self-marketers. The desire to put your best self forward isn't new. Prior to social media, record and book collections were your, "This is who I really am" ads.

Look, as I get older, I don't want to become one of those back in the "good old days" or "the world is worse" kinda gals. Honestly, I don't think people have changed, nor is it necessarily worse. I just believe our abilities to manipulate our images are easier and the impact greater. Before, we could only project our best selves to those we knew; you know, people who came to our homes. However, with the internet, we can now craft a perfect image and our cyber falsities can threaten to become our realities, a lie we can no longer manage. I blame bumper stickers. They were the gateway to this Pandora's box.

The problems with falsities are many. We forget that as we create the image of a perfect life, others are doing the same. The lives we see are someone's "highlight reel," and their images are often staged or manipulated. It is known that the highlight reel negatively impacts our emotional health: fear of missing out, social isolation, jealousy, disordered eating, depression, and self-loathing (or at least doubt). As well, our falsities might compel us to keep people at a distance through cyber-friendships or, at a minimum, friends kept away from anything that would blow our carefully crafted images. They are not invited home because then they would see how we actually live. You can't order what you really like to eat because you've told everyone you a vegetarian. You have to skip your reunion because even though you've aged, your image hasn't. You can't seek support for a struggling marriage or how to address a difficult issue with your kids because, well, everyone thinks it's all perfect. Little by little, the falsity claims your identity. It becomes an idol that requires sacrifices, one that will consume your emotional health and eventually your spiritual health.

Enter God. You are fully known. God knows you, the real you. He knows every hair on your head because He placed it there. He knows every thought, even the ones you barely allow yourself to think. He knows you read the tabloids, eat Frosted Flakes, binge watch *The Real Housewives*, and are grateful for

Minecraft. He knows the cellulite of your life, every bit of your brokenness and everything you believe makes you less. Yet despite being fully known, God fully loves you. He says you are beloved, worthy, beautiful, and treasured. When you are at your worst, His steadfast love remains, well, steadfast. If you are worried that who you are isn't good enough, then know God wants you exactly as you are and where you are. God doesn't want your highlight reel. He wants you. Like any loving parent, your heavenly Father is filled with the hope of you. He knows what you are called to. He knows you are able. He knows what is possible for your life. He doesn't need you to come to Him with your face washed and your life filtered. He doesn't want your falsities but your brokenness. Besides, it's really a waste of your time because God *knows* you.

God wants you to know He is sufficient. His plans for you are good. He wants to carry all the places you feel less. He wants you to experience the freedom and peace of knowing you can trust Him. God's got this. He's got you. He wants you to have steadfast faith in Him by surrendering all the broken. God wants you to know yourself as He knows you: sinful but forgiven, weak but made strong, broken but equipped, imperfect but fully known and fully loved.

God wants you to passionately make the image of Christ known through who He made you to be.

Reflection You know when I sit and when I rise; you perceive my thoughts from afar. You discern my going out and my lying down; you are familiar with all my ways. Before a word is on my tongue you, Lord, know it completely. (Psalm 139:2–4)

_____

_____

_____

_____

_____

_____

_____

_____

_____

_____

_____

_____

DAY 10

COMPLETE

And in Christ you have been brought
to fullness. He is the head over
every power and authority.

—Colossians 2:10

Goodness, don't you find that nagging sense of *want* annoying? For years I struggled with "wanting" and a sense of discontent. Look, I knew I was overwhelmingly blessed. I was raised by incredible parents, married my favorite human, gave birth to four healthy kids, and was financially secure. Nevertheless, I couldn't shake the wanting. I believe our wanting and discontent manifest themselves through unhealthy behaviors. For me, I didn't satisfy the want through buying things or busy-ness. But worse, I had crushing expectations of myself and my family, which caused a simmering impatience. During this season, I was attending church to support my husband—several years prior to my decision to give my life to Christ—another source of simmering impatience. Why did I have to get everyone ready for church? I often found myself wiping tears away, feeling exposed by God's Word. I hated how uncomfortable I felt. I hated crying (I don't cry). I hated that everyone around me seemed so at peace. I hated that I felt incomplete despite believing I had everything.

Knowing I was struggling with my identity as a mom, Chris signed us up for a parenting workshop led by Dr. Paul Tripp. Dr. Tripp said something that struck a chord in me so deep that I now know it was God's pursuit. (Just in case Dr. Tripp reads this, forgive me for this poor paraphrase. It's what my mushy, menopausal, mom-of-four brain remembers.)

> You were made to be an empty vessel with a deep want. Often to satisfy this deep want people get lost in the "bad" things of this world, like addiction, pornography, greed, and pride. Many of us, however, fill it with "good" things, like our marriage, our service to others, and even our children. But in both cases, the deep want remains. In both cases you are building false idols. Idols that can never satisfy. Why? God created you to desire Him above all. It is only when you fill yourself with God that you can experience the fullness for which you were created.

Cue the tears. In that moment I felt God speak directly to me. I knew my discontent—my want—would never be satisfied by my ample worldly blessings. Only through a relationship with God would I be satisfied. The nagging want I experienced was Jesus waiting patiently as God pursued me. Waiting for me to recognize that my good deeds, my blessings, and all my efforts would never fill the void. Without Christ, I could gain the world and have nothing. My nagging want was not a punishment; it was the gift of His persistent, quiet knock at the door to my heart. An invitation to ask for God's forgiveness and experience the fullness of His grace. A beckoning to surrender my life to Christ and follow Him.

The moment you surrender your life to Christ, you get a taste of the fullness. I remember that moment well. The peace of feeling complete. The world will convince you that self-reliance, constant toiling, and having "all the things" will make you complete. I promise it won't. You can be everything to everyone. You can have every possession you ever desired. You can be surrounded by admirers. You can achieve the body you've always believed would make you happy. You can have the best marriage, the best children, and the cleanest house. You can even be the best Christian. But you will still feel the want if you don't have an intimate relationship with God. And I don't know how that discontent will manifest itself in your life, but it will.

The good news is that the taste of fullness when Christ became your greatest desire is yours! You were made complete in Him. To experience your completeness ask yourself, "Am I, in this moment, this day, this week, this choice, living like Christ is my greatest desire? Am I seeking Him first, making Him my priority, and following His will?" You know the saying: "Show me where you spend your time and your money, and there you will find your greatest desire. Be second to Christ. Place your relationship with God above your marriage, your children, your work, and your personal goals. In a fallen world that sells so-called completeness and claims your identity, know that you are complete in Christ. Follow Him obediently; surrender your will to Him fully, and your life cannot help but produce fruit. Bonus: You will see the fruit you already have in a new light. In Christ you experience the truth: You are complete.

Reflection And in Christ you have been brought to fullness. He is the head over every power and authority. (Colossians 2:10)

_____

_____

_____

_____

_____

_____

_____

_____

_____

_____

_____

_____

_____

_____

FREE

> Because through Christ Jesus the law
> of the Spirit who gives life has set you
> free from the law of sin and death.
>
> —Romans 8:2

Do you live like one who has been set free? Romans 8:2 always reminds me of the parable of the sower. In Mark 4:18–19 (NLT), Jesus explains to the twelve:

> The seed that fell among the thorns represents others who hear God's word, but all too quickly the message is crowded out by the worries of this life, the lure of wealth, and the desire for other things, so no fruit is produced.

For years I've watched women—deeply rooted, faith-filled women—live among the thorns, imprisoned by the false worship of food. As a nutritionist, I used to say false worship of the diet culture, but the diet culture rebranded itself as "lifestyle," so now women immediately defend by saying their diet isn't a diet. It's a lifestyle. Although they seek God first in most of their lives, when it comes to what they eat and don't eat, they look to the messages of worldly gurus lured by the desire to see something different in the mirror or on the scale. They would not describe themselves as imprisoned. No, they are taking care of themselves. They would not describe their relationship with food as a false idol. Yet they live trembling in fear of certain foods (unclean, processed, refined) and bowing to the falsely elevated power of others (superfood, detoxifying, fat-burning, anti-inflammatory). In response to this, my business partner and I wrote a program the Common Sense Transformation (www.commonsensetransformation.com) to help heal women's relationships with food through developing a kingdom mindset in this area of their lives. We ask them to seek God's wisdom and strength in this area of their lives. We ask them to look upward so that they can finally experience God's freedom through the transformative power of the Holy Spirit.

Whether or not you struggle with your relationship with food, know that being saved and deeply rooted does not keep you immune to the lure of this fallen world or your own brokenness. On this side of heaven we all live in a briar patch. The problem is the thorns of this world and within ourselves are not always recognizably bad. The briar patch is often cleverly disguised. The enemy loves to deceive. He twists good desires or intentions into false idols and unaware willful disobedience. His weapons to draw you into the thorns are fear, worry, shame, and pride. When you allow fear, worry, shame, or pride to guide your choices, inevitably you turn from God's eternal truths to the ever-changing messages of this world (culture) and/or to self-reliance. Gazing downward and/or inward, you will not only stumble, you will participate in building your own prison walls.

Walls that separate you from God's protection, peace, and love. Walls that prevent you from producing fruit. Whether it is your marriage, your children, your weight, your wellness, your finances, your appearance, or any other area of your life you can think of, ask yourself if you seek God first. Have you surrendered your will and given up your expectation of, "If I do this, then I get (deserve) that"? Is this area of your life producing the fruits of the Spirit: love, joy, peace, patience, kindness, goodness, faithfulness, gentleness, and self-control (Galatians 5:22–23)?

God knows every briar patch in your path. He did not leave you to navigate this world alone! God's love for you nailed Jesus to the cross and covered you in His righteousness so you can live in intimate relationship with Him. God's goodness and faithfulness gave you the power of His indwelling Holy Spirit, a Spirit with transformative power. God's hope for you is to seek Him first in all things, so you can stand firm in His love, not be imprisoned by any briar patch in your life. Christ set you free. Through Him, you experience that freedom and its fruits.

Reflection Because through Christ Jesus the law of the Spirit who gives life has set you free from the law of sin and death. (Romans 8:2)

_____

_____

_____

_____

_____

_____

_____

_____

_____

_____

_____

_____

_____

_____

EQUIPPED

Now may the God of peace, who through
the blood of the eternal covenant brought
back from the dead our Lord Jesus, that
great Shepherd of the sheep, equip you
with everything good for doing his will,
and may he work in us what is pleasing
to him, through Jesus Christ, to whom
be glory forever and ever. Amen.

—Hebrews 13:20–21

Wow. If this verse doesn't bring you to your knees … God, through the blood of Jesus, equips you with everything good! "To do what?" you ask. Fair enough. Through the gift of the Holy Spirit, you are empowered to do God's will. Each time you obediently surrender and faithfully answer God's call, the Holy Spirit equips you to be a light in a broken world and bring glory to God.

In addition to my inability to be patient, I strive for perfection. By the fourth grade, my fear of not being perfect imprisoned me in an unwillingness to step up and try. My dad, seeing me struggle, would always say, "Carol, put down the weight of the finish line, and just take the next best step." He taught me to manage my fears. But I still felt inadequate no matter the outcome of my endeavors. For decades, without knowing what I was looking for, I searched for "something." I was drawn to church services, took religious classes in college, met with pastors to discuss what faith was and who Jesus is. Yet I never surrendered despite my growing, pressing need for Jesus. I never felt perfect enough, among some other obstacles. Then a friend I made at my husband's church said, "Carol, God doesn't call the equipped. He equips the called." I felt a weight lift. I didn't have to become perfect for God to use me; I just had to trust that He was sufficient and obey His call. When I finally said yes, my shortcomings—both real and perceived—didn't disappear. But with Jesus, I am able to be brave, assured in the knowledge that God has the finish line, and through Him, all things are possible.

Franklin D. Roosevelt once said, "Courage isn't the absence of fear, but rather the assessment that something else is more important than fear." God's plan for your life is more important than any fear you might have that keeps you from stepping out and stepping up. After I said yes to Jesus and surrendered my needs to His (ongoing), most people would describe me as a "fearless go-getter." Ha! Fearless? No. I battle my inadequacies every single day. But I know I no longer battle them alone. The confidence people see comes from my dependence on God. In every single situation that I set myself aside and choose to proceed with a willing, obedient heart, courageous faith, and reliance on His strength alone, God equips. I pray the confidence people see in me points them to Jesus.

You can absolutely trust that God will equip you. Every. Single. Time.

With Jesus, you are equipped to face your fears, endure your trials, overcome your insecurities, and be His light in a broken world. I don't know what your spiritual gifts are. Nor do I know what you will be called to do, but I promise you, as God's called, you will not be left to fend for yourself. He is with you. If God called you to the task, He will give you the grace and the tools required. Don't worry about the outcome. God's got that. All you need to do is take the next best step. Seek God first through the knowledge of His Word and prayer. Trust His plan and be obedient. Know that God has equipped you with spiritual gifts, and He has prepared you for whatever lies ahead. Break free of your fear, your inadequacies, and your will. Let go. Let God. Shine bright.

Reflection Now may the God of peace, who through the blood of the eternal covenant brought back from the dead our Lord Jesus, that great Shepherd of the sheep, equip you with everything good for doing his will, and may he work in us what is pleasing to him, through Jesus Christ, to whom be glory forever and ever. Amen. (Hebrews 13:20–21)

PURPOSED

"For I know the plans I have for you," declares
the Lord, "plans to prosper you and not to harm
you, plans to give you hope and a future."
—Jeremiah 29:11

How much of your God-given purpose is willingly or
unknowingly given to the enemy? Every day I arm myself
with Jeremiah 29:11. Truly. Whether it comes from my Jewish
heritage—the tradition of having God's words on the palms of
our hands, inscribed on our doors—-or not, I like the idea of
having Jeremiah 29:11 at hand (literally, an engraved bracelet)
before venturing into the battlefield of life. This verse reminds
me that every thought, every deed, and every word that comes
from my mouth *should* first be surrendered to God's will rather
than my own desires. And trust me when I tell you how often
I fail at this! I just repeat, "Thank You, God, for Your unfailing
grace."

I know Jeremiah 29:11 is perhaps one of the most popular life
verses and is often understood as a promise of a life without trial.

However, that understanding is mistaken. In its original context, Jeremiah was prophesying to the Israelites who were, in fact, up to their necks in trial! When Jeremiah sent God's declaration to the Israelites, they were being punished by God for their persistent rebellion. They were living in exile and enslavement to the Babylonians (Jeremiah 29:4–9). The promise of Jeremiah 29:11 comes only after God tells the Israelites that they must endure their suffering, pray to strengthen their relationship with the Lord Almighty, and finally turn their backs to false idols. In verse 10, God declares that their exile wasn't going to be short. He promises to restore His beloved people to their homeland but only after a period of seventy years. So an entire generation of Israelites knew they would die in exile.

Whew, just a bit of a contextual lesson! What is important is to understand that Jeremiah 29:11 does not promise that following God protects you from trial. Rather, it is the promise of an everlasting hope within the midst of it. Jeremiah 29:11 is the promise that when you surrender to God's will, follow and trust Him, He will give you the strength to persevere and endure any trial. He will use your suffering to draw you near so that you can overcome any trial—even death itself. Jeremiah 29:11 is the promise that when you pursue your God-given purpose in this world, your future is secure.

Persevere with hope. Trust that your current circumstance is not only momentary but God is using it for your good and His purposes. When you stand in faith at the foot of the cross and surrender to God's will for your life, then you experience His, "peace that surpasses all understanding." Like the generation of Israelites condemned to perish in Babylonia who were called to build lovely, purpose-driven, obedient lives despite their exile, you are called to live your life on the same foundation of hope in the promises of God, whether you experience them or not. Let your life be a witness to God's grace through your incomprehensible joy even in the pit of unhappiness. Live so filled with God's purpose that you are an undeniable light for the truth of Jesus. Live a life that is a testament to God.

Joy over despair.
Hope over bitterness.
Faith over fear.
Peace over anguish.
Purposed.

Reflection   "For I know the plans I have for you," declares the Lord, "plans to prosper you and not to harm you, plans to give you hope and a future." (Jeremiah 29:11)

_____

_____

_____

_____

_____

_____

_____

_____

_____

_____

_____

_____

_____

_____

EMPOWERED

> For this reason since the day we heard about
> you, we have not stopped praying for you.
> We continually ask God to fill you with the
> knowledge of his will through all the wisdom
> and understanding that the Spirit gives, so
> that you may live a life worthy of the Lord
> and please him in every way; bearing fruit in
> every good work, growing in the knowledge
> of God, being strengthened with all power
> according to his glorious might so that you
> may have great endurance and patience.
> —Colossians 1:9–11

Oh how I struggle to surrender to God's perfect will for my life. If you are anything like me, then surrender often looks like this: "Jesus take the wheel, but hey, don't mind me, I'm just gonna keep one hand on it in case you aren't going the way I want." My desire to surrender is rooted in my deep love for, and faith in, God, who wants only for my best. However, my desire to surrender often crashes at the intersection of, "Is this my will or

God's?" Do you ever feel like that? Please say yes so I feel better. The good news is Colossians 1:11 gives us a map, empowering us to know the way.

Can we just pause a bit before unpacking Colossians to give a quick thanks to God's servant Paul? The image of Paul relentlessly praying for me, praying for me to know God completely and to love Jesus above everything else—even my own worldly desires and selfish will—-is humbling and gives me great hope for my maturing ability to knowingly surrender. Thanks, Paul!

Okay, back to the subject at hand. Sure, in the big things—illness, marital/parenting/financial struggles—surrendering to Jesus feels easier. Right? I mean whenever I find myself nose-to-nose with life's biggest trials, I'm getting in the trunk and closing it shut, praying, "Jesus, Jesus, Jesus take control." See, I struggle to surrender the mundane little trials in life, the, "I can handle this," category of stuff. It's in the everyday speed bumps of life when seeking God's will first and surrendering to it gets tricky. Don't you find yourself grabbing for the wheel (or at least backseat driving) in those moments, forgetting to consult the road map (all the married ladies just chuckled a bit thinking of their hubbies) God gave us for our lives. Luckily, as well as praying for you, Paul is also the practical how-to apostle. He is the epitome of a great teacher. Paul not only lives what he teaches, but he breaks down how to surrender and discern in a way that is easily understood.

You: "Okay, so how do I know God's will so that I bear fruit, experience God's power, and am fueled by His strength to endure remaining patient in this trial?"

Paul: "Ask God to give you the knowledge of His will by *continually praying and reading His Word* so that His Spirit will give you wisdom and discernment. And just for good measure, know that I am over here praying for you as well" (Paul is always consulting the map, wink wink).

Wow. The phrase that comes to mind in light of Paul's teaching is, "It's not that complicated." So each time you feel the world-beating you down, each time you beat yourself up, every time you falter, doubt, fear or push and feel your strength draining from you … remember to follow Paul's example and heed his instructions. Paul patiently endured a life full of "big thing" trials because he was empowered by his faith in God's strength. Remember you are not asked to rely on your own strength but are "being strengthened" when you get in the trunk and surrender to God. Just bring your Bible and get busy praying. Seriously. God's will for your life is easily found. He has given you the power to discover the best route for your life: Just pick up your Bible. Read it. Read it again. And Pray. Ask for what you need, what you think you need, what you want. In this way, you surrender to your relationship with God by immersing yourself in His Word and praying continually. God filled you with Holy Spirit power to help you know Him better. The deeper you dive into His Word, the louder the Spirit's voice, and the more attuned you become to discern God's will for your life from your own, even in the mundane little things. The Holy Spirit will guide you and empower you with the gift of discernment when you seek God first. When you acknowledge that God's strength is sufficient and His will best, the more you experience His power to live your life in a way that is pleasing to God.

And oh, the fruit.

Reflection For this reason since the day we heard about you, we have not stopped praying for you. We continually ask God to fill you with the knowledge of his will through all the wisdom and understanding that the Spirit gives, so that you may live a life worthy of the Lord and please him in every way; bearing fruit in every good work, growing in the knowledge of God, being strengthened with all power according to his glorious might so that you may have great endurance and patience. (Colossians 1:9–11)

_____

_____

_____

_____

_____

_____

_____

_____

_____

_____

_____

DAY 15

ANOINTED

Now it is God who makes both us and
you stand firm in Christ. He anointed
us, set his seal of ownership on us, and
put his Spirit in our hearts as a deposit,
guaranteeing what is to come.
—2 Corinthians 1:21–22

Oh, what an encouraging, life-giving verse. Can't you just
hear this being delivered in a locker room at half-time? Your
opponent is powerful, the challenge daunting, but God has got
you. There is no force that can overtake you when you stand in
God's truth and follow His lead. Truly, what power can conquer
you with God on your side?

You are able to stand firm because you are anointed. Simply,
anointed means you are chosen and designated for a particular
purpose. Chosen by divine election to do what only you can
do! Your strengths and gifts are necessary parts of God's team.
In other words, get off the bench, and get out there. Play the
game of your life because God has anointed you! (Did anyone

else imagine *The 300*, locked in a phalanx, facing the Persian hoard? Just me, huh?)

Of course, the pre-game pep talk isn't the best part of God's anointing. The moment you surrendered your life to Christ, God filled you with His Spirit that flows through you. True, the Holy Spirit is a demonstration of God's saving grace, but it is also a constant source of God's empowerment. Anointed means God isn't just a coach on the sidelines but is *always* with you. His Spirit is whispering in your ear, instructing and guiding you through every challenge. (Okay, now I'm thinking about *The Matrix*.) The anointing is God in your heart, softening and strengthening you as needed. The anointing is God in your thoughts so that you grow in wisdom and think more like Christ. Anointed means no matter the opponent, your victory is assured.

So what kind of teammate are you? Are you trembling on the sidelines, praying you don't get put in the game? Or do you believe the success of the team relies solely on your abilities? Perhaps you are a game day only player, working only when others are watching. If you are like most people, myself included, you often find yourself struggling with aspects of each. Whenever I find myself not being all that God has anointed me to be in life or a specific situation, it is because I am not standing firm in Christ. I've put Christ on the bench. Luckily He waits patiently because He knows within each of us is the ability to be the best kind of teammate, an anointed player, one who works tirelessly when no one is watching; one who humbly and obediently desires to follow God's will, one who will set aside his or her own ambitions to best serve their teammates, one who knows their strengths are a gift from God given to fulfill His purposes.

One whose is sealed and stands firm.

Reflection Now it is God who makes both us and you stand firm in Christ. He anointed us, set his seal of ownership on us, and put his Spirit in our hearts as a deposit, guaranteeing what is to come. (2 Corinthians 1:21–22)

ROYAL PRIESTHOOD

But you are a chosen people, a royal priesthood,
a holy nation, God's special possession, that
you may declare the praises of Him who called
you out of darkness into his wonderful light.

—1 Peter 2:9

Called out. Set apart. A holy nation bound together by faith. A people who belong to God. His temple, living stone built on the sure foundation of Christ. But you are also His royal priesthood. The definition of priest is, "one especially consecrated to the service of a divinity and through whom worship, prayer, sacrifice, or other service is offered to the object of worship." In the Old Testament, God established a covenantal agreement with the Levites and the descendants of Aaron. They were ordained by God as His *mediators* to the people.

But Jesus! Through the suffering, death, and resurrection of Jesus Christ, all who believe and follow are now God's priests. When Peter wrote to Christians scattered across Asia Minor, he was encouraging them to stand firm as believers. First Peter 2:9 is a reminder that you are in this world but not of it; you have been chosen by God before the foundation of the world, set apart to be His. You, my friend, were worth dying for. In light of this truth, let your faith, your life, proclaim Christ. You are called to be God's mediator to the world.

So as God's royal priesthood, what exactly is your job description? First, praise God and proclaim the truth of Jesus Christ. You are empowered to share the gospel and advance His mission. However, remember that you were not ordained because of your own actions but through the undeserved gift of grace. My dad always taught me, "To whom much is given, much is required." In other words, your salvation comes with responsibilities. Your second task is to love God's people. Honor God by living like Christ, a life that ministers and serves His people. You are not to stand in judgment of others but are called to invite the broken into your life, to love others as Christ loved you. To show them the beauty, the comfort, the joy, and the peace of choosing to die to self and live for Christ. You, as a royal priest, are called to care for all of God's people. To be a blessing to others. To lift others through service, to see a need and fill a need, and to live a life where you are the hands and feet of Christ. Your job is to proclaim the truth and love others to glorify God.

And if like me you feel unworthy to be called a royal priesthood, remember God does not call the perfect. He equips the broken, sin-filled but made clean, undeserving but forgiven, hopeless but now hope itself, disobedient but loved, weak but made strong, unrighteous but covered. Christ is sufficient. Your brokenness serves as a testament to the depth of God's grace.

Trust that once a refugee, you are now God's special possession. You have been called out to live a life that declares God's glory so that others can find their way home. Together, a holy nation bound together by faith.

Reflection   But you are a chosen people, a royal priesthood, a holy nation, God's special possession, that you may declare the praises of Him who called you out of darkness into his wonderful light. (1 Peter 2:9)

_____

_____

_____

_____

_____

_____

_____

_____

_____

_____

_____

_____

_____

Know you are the love of God's life.

FORGIVEN

> "Come now, let us settle the matter," says
> the Lord. "Though your sins are like scarlet,
> they shall be as white as snow; though they
> are red as crimson, they shall be like wool."
> —Isaiah 1:18

The cost of your redemption was the precious blood of Jesus Christ. The gift of God's forgiveness was freely given but at such an unimaginable cost. When God asked Abraham to sacrifice his son, God stayed his hand. But He willingly sacrificed His own beloved Son for us who, quite frankly, are wholly undeserving. When I am feeling a bit full of myself, a bit undone by the world, or frustrated with God, I remember Jesus. Fully God, Jesus was aware of the coming suffering. Fully human, Jesus was aware of the excruciating pain of death by crucifixion. Innocent, Jesus remained fully surrendered. Growing up, every Easter my family watched *Jesus of Nazareth*. Even the umpteenth time I watched the movie, I would angrily wave my chocolate bunny at the screen and yell at Jesus, "Come on! Defend yourself!" As a Jewish kid, I would think, *If you are the Messiah, then destroy*

Your enemies. Right? Then as the sky grows dark, in Jesus's final moment, He looks to God and utters, "Father forgive them. They know not what they do." As crazy as it sounds, I think that cheesy seventies film planted the first seeds in my own redemption story.

How? Why? To love people so fully,

Forgive them. For they know not what they do.

God is a God of forgiveness. Throughout the Bible, He consistently chooses to forgive. He gives us paradise. We are not satisfied. He reveals Himself through wonders and miracles. Still we grumble, question, and demand. He fights our battles, sets us apart, and never breaks His covenant. Yet we remain willful, disobedient, and turn to the idols of self and the things of this world. He gives us every opportunity to turn from our sins, but we are unwilling. What, then, is God's choice? He could so easily breathe our destruction and start fresh. But no. God's faithful love is more powerful than sin. God chooses to take on flesh, step down from His throne in heaven, and enter the world as a vulnerable baby with no pedigree or power. Throughout His life, Jesus served God's people. He revealed Himself through miracles. But more often than not, He simply taught the truth, loved others, and honored His Father. Still they accused Him. Tried Him. Crucified Him.

And then He humbly and quietly fought *the* battle. The battle to once and for all conquer death, the enemy, and redeem us. He fought through surrender. He fought through obedience. He fought through love. The grave was not conquered on the battlefield but on the cross. The enemy and our sins were not vanquished through might but by Jesus's humility and God's choice to forgive.

God knows you know not what you do. Yet His love is so unfathomable that He chose to forgive, redeeming you and covering you in His righteousness. His forgiving grace is an ocean with no floor; it is a cleansing rain that never ceases. Neither you nor I can ever earn the gift of forgiveness and salvation. Jesus covered you. He covered me. He chose to willingly suffer and die so that His Father can forgive and redeem. Oh, to be loved so fully.

And yet washed in God's forgiving grace, we still wonder about our worth. Sister, I am here to tell you, you are worth stepping down from a heavenly throne, taking on flesh, and giving up all power. You are worth every lash from the whip, every thorn, and the weight of every sin while He gasped for breath on the cross. You are worth the indignity of an undeserved death to which He willingly submitted. You are not forgiven because of who you are but because of who God is. The cost of this unimaginable forgiveness:

**Choose Jesus.
Follow Him.**

Reflection "Come now, let us settle the matter," says the Lord. "Though your sins are like scarlet, they shall be as white as snow; though they are red as crimson, they shall be like wool." (Isaiah 1:18)

_____

_____

_____

_____

_____

_____

_____

_____

_____

_____

_____

_____

_____

DAY 18

LOVED

For God so loved the world that He gave His
one and only Son, that whoever believes in
Him shall not perish but have eternal life.

—John 3:16

You are loved. Beyond measure. Beyond comprehension. Worth fighting for. Worth forgiving. Worth dying for. Of all God's beautiful creations, He set you apart as His treasured possession. Breathe that in for a moment. If you are anything like me, then you need to hear the truth of God's love on the daily.

As you all know by now, I was raised in a Jewish family but surrendered my life to Christ at the age of forty. I believed in God. I believed in being a good person (a mensch). In fact, I believed so deeply that I was a good person it was a barrier to surrendering to Jesus. After reading the New Testament for the first time, a found connection between Exodus and John weakened my barrier. In Exodus God's love for me seemed stern, distant, and conditional. As a kid, I believed God's message was clear: Earn God's love through your actions. I believed I was good. I didn't break any of the Ten Commandments (at least not the big ones). I was grateful for the manna in my life. In fact, I was the kind of girl who would share the manna. So why didn't I feel "good enough"? My greatest fear, which held my feet to what I believed was the good path, was the thought, *What if I'm not good enough?*

Jesus broke through to me in John. God's love cannot be earned. Jesus was an undeserved gift, a gift that carried my sins and makes me good enough. God's love is not stern, distant, or conditional. In fact, it is a steadfast love that is freely given. The manna I received from God was so much more than physical sustenance; it was grace raining down to cover me in God's righteousness and satisfy my most important need—my spiritual wellness—to receive God's forgiveness and be in an eternal relationship with Him. Suddenly Jesus was the manna for me, scattered everywhere in my life. I had to choose to pick it up each and every day. I had to choose to receive the truth about the depth of God's love for me. I have to choose daily to live through and by that love. I have to choose to share that love with others.

Both Exodus and John have a simple message: Believe. Believe God's love will abundantly provide. Believe that His love cannot be earned through your actions because it was before you were born. Believe that God's love is absolutely faithful and steadfast. So much so that He, "gave His one and only Son," despite your brokenness. Believe that Jesus's life, crucifixion, death, and resurrection make up God's personal invitation to live in love with Him for all eternity.

Know you are the love of God's life.

I have loved you, my people, with an everlasting love. With unfailing love I have drawn you to myself. (Jeremiah 31:3)

Know that God's love is sufficient. Yes, you are loved beyond measure. Beyond comprehension. Worth dying for. Forgiven. Enough. Know that once you choose to receive the gift of God's love and surrender to it, it is transformative.

Reflection For God so loved the world that He gave His one and only Son, that whoever believes in Him shall not perish but have eternal life. (John 3:16)

_____

_____

_____

_____

_____

_____

_____

_____

_____

_____

_____

_____

_____

_____

VICTORIOUS

But thanks be to God! He gives us the
victory through our Lord Jesus Christ.
—1 Corinthians 15:57

Do you live a triumphant life? I ask in all earnestness, do you? Do I? If I am honest, sometimes, and sometimes not so much. But I want to live a life that is *always* from the certainty of Christ's victory. I know that we have not only been delivered from the guilt of sin but also from its power over us. I know that we live awash in the grace of Jesus nailed to the cross and in the assurance of His grave-conquering resurrection. I know that Jesus's crucifixion and His resurrection were not to overturn a defeat. There is no need to analyze a replay. Nor is there an asterisk by the W. Rather, Jesus's suffering, death, and resurrection are the manifestations of God's victory. In fact, the resurrection of Jesus Christ is the greatest victory in the history of the world. It is God's gift of grace breaking in on a fallen world and freeing humans once and for all from sin's bondage.

The first question: What does a victorious life like that look like? We all must first understand that it is not our victory we celebrate—no dancing obnoxiously in the end zone. Rather, God's victory is a gift. More important, this gift is wholly underserved and cannot be earned. So living a life of victory is a lot about your posture. When you realize you live a life in Christ's end zone, the response is to give thanks and praise God daily for loving you so completely that He stepped down from His throne in heaven and became man. It's a life knowing everything we have is God's, and everything we are is for His purpose and glory. It's a life of surrendering to the truth that our victory is not a result of our strength but God's alone. It is a life of confident humility.

The second question: How do you live a life in the certainty of Christ's victory? When I was a kid, I was gobsmacked in science when my teacher said, "If you find yourself in quicksand [I grew up in a time when the threat of quicksand was a real and present danger], stop struggling! Struggling only makes you sink faster." In college, getting certified to be a lifeguard, the lesson of struggling was once again taught: "Be aware that often the greatest danger of rescuing a drowning person is when they fight." For me, these early life lessons remain a constant part of my maturing faith: "Carol, stop struggling and wrestling God for control." I love how God constantly teaches how to live in the certainty of His victory through the everyday aspects of our lives (well, not quicksand … still have never seen any despite my childhood belief that it was everywhere). The *how* of a victorious life is simple: Trust.

The lesson: God wants you to live in His victory and assurance. God's got you. He's got your circumstance, your fear, and your doubt. Just stop struggling! Stop battling your rescuer against the quicksand in your life. Stop battling the lifeguards (His Word, His Spirit, His presence, sisters/brothers in Christ) God places in your life to keep you from drowning. Give Him dominion over your life through praising Him, daily prayer, reading His Word, and sharing His good news. When you find yourself in quicksand, be still. Remember, Christ's victory was realized by seeking His Father's will, knowing His Word, and trusting His Father's plan. To experience God's victory, surrender your life!

Reflection But thanks be to God! He gives us the victory through our Lord Jesus Christ. (1 Corinthians 15:57)

_____

_____

_____

_____

_____

_____

_____

_____

_____

_____

_____

_____

_____

REDEEMED

In Him we have redemption through his
blood, the forgiveness of sins, in accordance
with the riches of God's grace that he
lavished on us. With all wisdom and
understanding, He made known to us the
mystery of His will according to His good
pleasure, which He purposed in Christ.
—Ephesians 1:7–9

You are redeemed. The definition of redeem is to buy back,
to get back; to free from captivity by payment of ransom, to
help overcome, to release from blame or debt, to free from
the consequence of sin, to change for the better, to repair
and make good. The price of your redemption is the precious
blood of Christ. Charles Spurgeon wrote that our redemption
is not through the power or love of Christ but through Christ's
blood. Jesus traded His blood for your life. He purchased your
deliverance from the bondage of sin, and you are now a citizen
of God's kingdom.

You are restored. Rescued from darkness to be a part of God's family. Through Jesus's blood, God revealed His plan to reclaim all who trust in Christ to glorify Him. Your redemption is the revelation of God's grace for you through Jesus. I pray you swim in this truth! You belong to God, and in Him you will find nothing but acceptance, forgiveness, love, freedom, goodness, and the truth that you are exactly who you need to be: the love of God's life.

From Genesis to Revelation, the Bible tells the story of God's plan to restore and redeem what is His. His intention is for you to experience a part of your redemption during your earthly life. Yes, to experience God's love, power, righteousness, justice, and grace through an intimate, personal relationship with Him. Paul understood that the gift of the Holy Spirit was a seal of God's grace, a down payment for all you will experience in your future eternal inheritance. God's desire is for you to live the life He intended for you, a life overflowing with God's peace, strength, truth, and grace.

Through the world and our flesh, the enemy seeks to destroy the you God intended you to be. If he cannot destroy it, his backup plan is to diminish you. However, through the blood of Jesus, God rescued you from the enemy's plan. He provided the way for you to break free and filled you with His Spirit to help. God is no longer a distant deity but is present and constantly revealing Himself to you in personal ways. He desires to satisfy your every need, to refresh your spirit, and to be a source of incomprehensible peace even in the midst of your worst struggle. He wants to free you from your fears and be your strength when you face them. He wants you to know you never have to battle alone. Your heavenly Father stands between you and every temptation that seeks to pull you from His love. He is your strong tower. He wants you to walk in His truth, trusting that His love bears your wandering heart. He steadfastly believes and hopes that you will walk in His ways and will endure your failings. God wants you to experience His grace as He continuously works for your good. He wants you to cling to the truth that his, "grace is sufficient for you, for [His] power is made perfect in weakness." When you experience His peace, rely on His strength, trust Him completely; you are a living testimony of His grace. Who or what can stand against you?

You were rescued to do great things. You were redeemed because you are worth more to God than you can ever comprehend.

Reflection In Him we have redemption through his blood, the forgiveness of sins, in accordance with the riches of God's grace that he lavished on us. With all wisdom and understanding, He made known to us the mystery of His will according to His good pleasure, which He purposed in Christ. (Ephesians 1:7–9)

_____

_____

_____

_____

_____

_____

_____

_____

_____

_____

_____

_____

HIS

> Shout for joy to the Lord, all the earth. Worship
> the Lord with gladness; come before him with
> joyful songs. Know that the Lord is God. It
> is he who made us, and we are his; we are his
> people, the sheep of his pasture. Enter his gates
> with thanksgiving and his courts with praise;
> give thanks to him and praise his name. For the
> Lord is good and his love endures forever; his
> faithfulness continues through all generations.
>
> —Psalm 100

One of my favorite truths about God: He pursues. God chases after His people. He is the good shepherd who relentlessly seeks the lost. When you wander, He doesn't just wait for you to reverse course and return to Him. No. Every single time He finds you! One lost sheep breaks God's heart. One lost sheep is one too many. He wants what is His, and you, my friend, are His.

What does belonging to God mean? What does that look like in everyday life? I can tell you from personal experience, the choice to belong to yourself and be completely self-reliant is a heavy burden. The moment you surrender to Christ and recognize that you are not your own, your strength is not sufficient, your "goodness" is not enough, your "badness" doesn't make you unworthy, and your emptiness is actually your need for Jesus (yes, even after you are saved). You feel the burden lifted, and you experience that "peace that surpasses all understanding." Recognizing that you are His—handing the burden of who you are, who you pretend to be, or who you want to be over to Jesus—is freeing and transformative.

Remember God pursues what is His. He not only pursues those sheep that are lost, but as a good shepherd, He continues to provide, guide, and protect. Even in the midst of your greatest trial, when the enemy seeks to steal you from God, remember whose you are. Remember that God has poured His Spirit into you. Pray for God to fight your battles and carry the burden. Seek His wisdom, and allow the Holy Spirit to convict you to what is the right choice. Know that His love is a source of comfort. In every trial, no matter the outcome, trust in God's faithfulness. The choice to belong to God by asking Jesus to be the Lord of your life makes you His. But to fully experience what that means, you must choose to follow through prayer, through reading His Word, and through surrender. The more you surrender your life and your willful self-reliance to God, the more completely you experience the joy of being His.

God speaks often to how He knows us. Through Jesus, God welcomes you to know Him intimately. Do not settle for just hoping you belong to God, something I did for years. Know that you are His through ignited faith. Run to His voice when He calls you from the darkness. Run to His arms as they are always ready to embrace. Be still to hear His Spirit. Surrender to His will for your life. Remember that ignited faith empowers you to experience the fullness of God's joy and peace.

God pursues what is His.

Each day it is up to you to pursue Him just as relentlessly. Know that you are His. See yourself through His eyes. Then you will live like you are His, and your life will be transformed.

Reflection Shout for joy to the Lord, all the earth. Worship the Lord with gladness; come before him with joyful songs. Know that the Lord is God. It is he who made us, and we are his; we are his people, the sheep of his pasture. Enter his gates with thanksgiving and his courts with praise; give thanks to him and praise his name. For the Lord is good and his love endures forever; his faithfulness continues through all generations. (Psalm 100)

ABOUT THE AUTHOR

Carol Bevil is cofounder of Fuel Your Body, Feed Your Soul (FYBFYS), a God-first approach to nutrition, body image, and food relationship. FYBFYS is founded on Romans 12:2 and focuses on renewing the mind before transforming the body.

Carol is wife to Chris (twenty-three years), mother to four (Will, twenty; Hannah, eighteen; Katherine, twelve; Olivia, ten), personal trainer, and a cycling performance and nutrition coach. She has been in the health and fitness industry for more than thirty years. She holds multiple certifications in cycling, personal training, and nutrition and has dedicated her career to helping others believe all things are possible. Years of coaching and seeing the diet and wellness industry become false idols, destroying women's peace and stealing their joy, led her to create FYBFYS, a place where Tuesday transformation is uprooted and replaced with the biblical truth of Romans 12:2.

Carol was raised in a Jewish family but felt Jesus's pursuit the whole of her life. Stubborn and willful, she begrudgingly attended church with her husband and constantly pestered the pastor. One Sunday he challenged her to read the Old Testament and look for Jesus. There He was, on every page. She was baptized at the age of forty and has spent the last thirteen years doing her best to surrender her willful spirit (sometimes multiple times each hour).

Printed in the United States
by Baker & Taylor Publisher Services